NOIR
Erasure
Poetry
Anthology

NOIR

ERASURE POETRY ANTHOLOGY

EDITED BY

MELANIE VILLINES

CONTRIBUTING EDITORS

JENNI B. BAKER

CATFISH MCDARIS

JAMES W. MOORE

GERALD SO

COVER ART

GUY BUDZIAK

SILVER BIRCH PRESS
LOS ANGELES, CALIFORNIA

ISBN-13: 978-0615924137

ISBN-10: 0615924131

FIRST EDITION, December 2013

Email: silver@silverbirchpress.com

Web: silverbirchpress.com

Blog: silverbirchpress.wordpress.com

Book Design: Silver Birch Press

Cover Art: Guy Budziak, filmnoirwoodcuts.com.

Mailing Address:
Silver Birch Press
P.O. Box 29458
Los Angeles, CA 90029

The Silver Birch Press
NOIR ERASURE POETRY ANTHOLOGY
is dedicated to
Raymond Chandler

INTRODUCTION

MELANIE VILLINES

As a longtime fan of hardboiled detective fiction and film noir, and an aficionado of found poetry, I wondered what would happen if the two were combined. A call for submissions on the Silver Birch Press blog, as well as requests from our contributing editors to their colleagues resulted in a wide range of submissions, including those featured in this volume.

So just what is an erasure poem? Take a page from any book, cross out or whiteout some of the words and the remaining words constitute the erasure poem. The Silver Birch Press *Noir Erasure Poetry Anthology* pays homage to noir authors— including genre founders Raymond Chandler and Dashiell Hammett, as well as other authors of crime fiction whose work served as source material—and falls under the umbrella of fair use. To the best of our ability, we have obscured the redacted words to make the original volume unrecognizable. It is our intention to focus on the few words that remain from the original—thereby creating something new.

A few poets featured in the collection selected work outside the noir mainstream, but I made an exception for various reasons—including the desire to give the collection greater balance by adding women authors, as well as including younger authors and featuring some genre crossovers.

My thanks to the forty-six poets represented in this collection, as well as the sixteen authors whose writing served as inspiration. A special thank you to contributing editors Jenni B. Baker, Catfish McDaris, james w. moore, and Gerald So— accomplished poets and authors who encouraged their writing colleagues to participate in the collection. Special thanks to Guy Budziak of filmnoirwoodcuts.com for the book's beautiful cover image.

Noir and erasure poetry are a perfect match—stark, pared down, elemental, bare bones. As the author who invented L.A. Noir and elevated prose to poetry, we dedicate this volume to Raymond Chandler.

NOIR AUTHORS

NOIR POETS

"The streets were dark
with something more than night."
RAYMOND CHANDLER

a fine girl ▓▓▓▓▓▓

▓▓▓▓▓▓▓▓▓▓▓▓▓▓▓▓▓▓ I been pounding
the pavements ▓▓▓▓▓▓▓▓▓▓▓▓▓▓▓▓▓▓. I
couldn't get to sleep ▓▓▓▓▓▓

▓▓▓▓▓▓▓▓▓▓▓ I'd love ▓▓▓▓▓▓ a break.
▓▓▓ I got expenses to meet, ▓▓▓▓▓▓

▓▓▓▓▓▓▓▓▓▓▓▓▓▓▓▓▓▓▓▓▓▓▓

▓▓▓▓▓▓▓▓▓▓▓ If you ▓▓▓▓▓▓▓▓
come home with me. ▓▓▓▓▓▓▓

▓▓▓▓▓▓▓▓▓▓▓▓▓▓▓▓▓▓▓▓▓

▓▓▓▓▓▓▓▓▓▓▓▓▓▓▓▓▓▓▓

▓▓▓▓ across the alley. ▓▓▓▓▓▓▓

▓▓▓▓▓▓▓▓▓▓▓▓▓▓▓▓▓▓▓▓▓

▓▓▓ no more time to waste. ▓▓▓▓▓

▓▓▓▓▓▓▓▓▓▓▓▓▓▓▓▓

▓▓▓▓▓▓▓▓▓▓▓▓▓▓▓▓▓▓▓

"Joey, where ▓ you going?" ▓▓▓▓▓▓

▓▓▓▓▓▓▓▓▓▓▓▓▓▓

"Pretty please ▓▓▓▓▓▓▓
"Pretty please," ▓▓▓▓

Jeffrey C. Alfier

A fine girl

I been pounding the pavements.

I couldn't get to sleep.

I'd love a break.

I got expenses to meet.

If you come home with me

across the alley—

no more time to waste.

Joey, where you going?

Pretty please. Pretty please.

Blue City by Ross Macdonald
Chapter 11

Listen.

I've tried to
time
The   silence
the

narrow

pose   the
wait
the night
stared

down   the   second

minutes
dance   around the
mess   way out

past

the writing   and   into
the pen

14

Beth Ayer

Point

Listen.
I've tried to
time the silence
the narrow pose
the wait
the night stared down
the second
minutes dance around
the mess
way out
past the writing
and into the pen

"Smart-Aleck Kill" by Raymond Chandler

You   get used

to

relapses   the people you

like

turn

cheap   pawn

hope

for

experience

take what's offered and

sip

the stuff

of feeling

Jenni B. Baker

Relapses

You get used to relapses
the people you like turn cheap
pawn hope for experience
take what's offered
and sip the stuff of feeling.

The Long Goodbye by Raymond Chandler
Chapter 2

46

the eyeballs,

can't do anything

Get your

head just barely

sick.

the girl

pressed

a little more to the side

his eyes,

said slowly

Things

unscrupulous, have been done

hurting people.

further.

"The cards are dealt,"

a little. Suddenly

forlorn man

said softly.   The last flicker of

the ham.

18

David Barker

the cards are dealt

the eyeballs
can't do anything.

get your head
just barely sick.

the girl pressed
a little more
to the side.

his eyes said slowly
"things unscrupulous
have been done,
hurting people
further."

"the cards are dealt,"
a suddenly forlorn man
said softly.

the last flicker of
the ham.

"Pickup On Noon Street" by Raymond Chandler

a yellowish
rope

He

fell
wooden-faced

blood spurted out

his   eyes
were wide open

body was   still

his

body was   still   his

his

hand   would touch nothing

The eyes
frozen
extinguished

Kathy Burkett

At the End of His Rope

A yellowish
   rope.
He
  fell
    wooden-faced.
        Blood spurted out.

His   eyes
were wide open.
His   body
was still.

His   hand
would touch nothing.

The eyes
frozen,
extinguished.

The Maltese Falcon by Dashiell Hammett
Chapter 16

. There was ▮▮▮▮▮ her smile. ▮▮▮▮▮

like a fairy, ▮▮▮▮▮

▮▮▮ silver fingernails ▮▮▮ blond hair ▮▮▮ come in tomorrow. ▮▮▮ be here tomorrow▮

▮▮▮ eyes narrowed ▮▮▮ a faint greenish glitter, ▮▮▮ the shadow of trees. ▮▮▮ chopped off a breath.

▮▮▮ her face fell apart ▮▮▮ The smile came back, with a couple of corners badly bent.

▮▮▮ come in ▮ tomorrow▮

▮▮▮ pale-faced and tight-lipped▮

▮▮▮ 'Tomorrow, ▮▮▮ a faint sucking noise ▮▮▮ the corner ▮▮▮ the alley ▮ ▮▮▮ the stores▮ ▮▮▮ with wire sides ▮ ▮▮▮ the boulevard ▮▮▮ the block ▮▮▮ A fresh-faced kid ▮ reading ▮▮▮ a dollar▮

Candace Butler

Tomorrow

There was her smile.
like a fairy,
silver fingernails   blond hair
come in
Tomorrow. be here tomorrow.
eyes narrowed   a faint greenish glitter
the shadow of trees
chopped off breath.

her face fell apart
The smile came back, with a couple of corners
badly bent.
come in tomorrow
pale-faced
and tight-lipped

Tomorrow,
a faint
sucking noise
the corner   the alley
the stores   with wire sides
the boulevard
the block

A fresh-faced kid reading
a dollar

The Big Sleep by Raymond Chandler
Chapter 1

money

rich

wife

jazzy week-end,   wearing

                                    time and information
A   sedan   from ■■ City Hall.

TWENTY-ONE

■■ a gusty wind blowing

                                                    roll-
ing across   like

                                            life
                                    took a drink

                                            polite
                        feeling

■Yes,

                                    photographs

                                            a number of times
last night
    ■I was ■■ getting drunk

            five hundred dollars. Will that be satisfactory?

Freda Butler

Twenty-One

Money
rich wife
jazzy week-end, wearing
time and information
a sedan from City Hall.

A gusty wind blowing
rolling across
like
life
took a drink.

Polite
feeling
yes,
photographs
a number of times last night.

I was getting drunk
five hundred dollars. Will that be satisfactory?

The Big Sleep by Raymond Chandler
Chapters 20 & 21

Something

black dark

on the stairs,

laying there

in the water

Kim Cooper

Something

Something

           black dark

         on the stairs,

             laying there

in the water

The Postman Always Rings Twice by James M. Cain
Chapter 4

I WAS ███████████████ ████████ at the office. ███████

I was feeling ████████ ██████████████ fit. ████,
██
██
██
██
██████████████████████████. Getting out of
bed ████████████████████ facing the blank wall
██
██
██
██

But trouble ████████████ kept a man alive. ████
trying to avoid ████████████ a full time job. ████
sometimes ████ in sleep █████████████████████
██
██
██
██ t
███
████ you are ████████████████████████████████
██
████████████████ either frightened ████ or ████
██
████████████████████████████████ It's only
a dream about a big elephant ████████████████
██
██

Subhankar Das

A Big Elephant

I was at the office
I was feeling
getting out of bed facing the blank wall.
But trouble kept a man alive
trying to avoid a full time job.
Sometimes in sleep
you are either frightened
or it's only a dream about
a big elephant.

Pulp by Charles Bukowski
Chapter 26

the cigarette set fire to

forgotten

disgust. shot a forty-four or forty-five

across the street Nobody

was wearing

Nothing except a weck

Alone

on

his lips

a careless circle

with yellow-grey eyes

looking dissatisfied

eyes hard as green pebbles

turned to the table

Andrea Janelle Dickens

Alone

The cigarette set fire to
forgotten disgust.

Shot a forty-four
or forty-five across

the street. Nobody
was wearing nothing—

except a week. Alone
on his lips a careless circle

with yellow-grey eyes
looking dissatisfied

eyes hard as green pebbles
turned to the table.

The Maltese Falcon by Dashiell Hammett
Chapter 2

"He oughtn't to have shot at you,"

"If you want to know about guts, try being a small-town chief of police some day."

on Arguello Boulevard

like a coyote howl—

A siren wailed

ing in the hills.

De Spain

shot from his pocket with the white-handled gun he

The slug went a foot

over my head

twice

shot

The chief

"This one's alive." he snapped.

Barbara Eknoian

Bay City Blues

De Spain shot from his pocket
with the white handled gun.
The slug went a foot
over my head.
The chief shot twice.
"This one's alive,"
he snapped.
He oughn't to have shot out."
"If you want to know
about guts, try being
a small-town chief of police
some day."
A siren wailed
on Arguello Boulevard
like a coyote howling
in the hills.

"Bay City Blues" by Raymond Chandler

I   wanted
              the
                 hundred   lonely

                                    things:

his   pocket

          a small button   a
              maze

     daylight   an exposed

                              door.

                        "Hello,

Remember me?" I said.

     I   put the key in

Chris Forhan

Erasing Sleep

I   wanted
        the
           hundred   lonely

                things:

his   pocket

    a small button   a
    maze

daylight   an exposed

             door.

        "Hello,"

Remember me" I said.

I   put the key in

The *Big Sleep* by Raymond Chandler
Chapter 11

ON ▪

It was about ▮▮▮▮▮
▮▮▮▮▮ a look of ▮▮▮▮
▮ clearness ▮▮▮▮▮▮
▮▮▮▮▮▮▮▮
▮▮▮▮▮▮▮▮
▮▮▮ neat, clean, ▮▮▮
▮▮▮▮▮ everything ▮▮
▮▮▮▮▮▮▮ on
▮▮▮▮
The main ▮▮▮▮▮
stories ▮▮▮▮▮ have
let ▮ a ▮▮▮▮▮
stain ▮▮▮ show ▮▮ in ▮▮
▮▮▮▮▮▮▮
▮▮ some ▮▮▮▮▮
▮▮ push ▮▮▮▮▮ to be
▮▮▮ fiddling with ▮ knots on ▮ ropes
▮▮▮▮▮ and not getting anywhere.

36

Laura Hartenberger

On

It was about
            a look of
clearness

            neat, clean,
                    everything
                        on.

The main
stories   have
let a
stain   show   in

            some
            push to be
            fiddling with knots on ropes
                    and not getting anywhere.

The Big Sleep by Raymond Chandler
Chapter 1

. His
eyes had a shine
grey   like a statue,

a
e street,
man
that hat,   that frame.

across
the gutter
a   keening
rat.

splay-
footed
Silence.

I could have sat in

Paul Hawkins

Framed

His eyes	had a shine
grey	like a statue
a street	man
that hat	that frame
across	the gutter
a	keening rat

splay-footed silence

| I could | have sat in. |

Farewell My Lovely by Raymond Chandler
Chapter 2

The knuckles hit   deep

"You son of a bitch,"

I hit   with my left hand.
The pillow
drifted slow as a piece of tissue paper

I sprawled across the floor. I caught one of his
ankles and rolled over with it, bringing him down on me,

Men came in and dragged us apart.

One of the coppers laughed. "Jesus," he said admiringly, "there's a
woman with hair on her chest."

I said I didn't think it was much

A lot of blood

"Tough luck.

get a doctor

put a towel over the wound

Deborah Herman

A Woman with Hair
on Her Chest

The knuckles hit deep "You son of a bitch"
I hit with my left hand, the pillow drifted slow as a
piece of tissue paper.
I sprawled across the floor. I caught one of his ankles
and rolled
over with it, bringing him down on me.
Men came in and dragged us apart.
"You didn't have to knock me cold."
One of the coppers laughed. "Jesus," he said
admiringly, "there's a woman
with hair on her chest."
I said I didn't think it was much. A lot of blood.
"Tough luck." Get a doctor.
I put a towel over the wound. Don't let's fuss over it.

The Thin Man by Dashiell Hammett
Chapter 24

and

Miles slid down and

turned ⬛ put a leg over the fence.

and looked back ⬛ with sur-

prised ⬛ eyes.

"His gun

was supposed to be

in his pocket

---

fell away steeply to the

dark ground

Street below.

Fifteen feet down the

slope

Two men stood over

the dead man.

One of them

clambered up to the

alley, his shadow running up the slope.

He was a barrel-bellied

man with shrewd small eyes,

carelessly

he stepped over the broken fence.

took a fat revolver from his

coat-pocket

That's it.

"Yes," he said,

then ⬛ rapidly;

"Let's him have it

Sandra Herman

bad business

dark ground fell away steeply to the street below
fifteen feet down the slope
two men stood over
the dead man
one of them
clamoured up the alley
his shadow running up the slope
he was a barrel-bellied
man with shrewd small eyes

carelessly
he stepped over the broken fence
took a fat revolver from his coat-pocket
"yes," he said
"that's it"
then rapidly
lets him have it

and
Miles slid down and
turned
put a leg over the fence
and looked back
with surprised eyes
his gun
was supposed to be
in his pocket

The Maltese Falcon by Dashiell Hammett
Chapter 2

I. Spade & Archer

under
back to
horizontal
    outward from   above
        down-from

        tan
clung   brown
          face   shutting
    leaned against

     so
knockout
   Shoo   Shoo
                        back
     standing   hand

        advanced slowly
tentative steps   cobalt-blue eyes
    probing.

Mathias Jansson

Knockout Words

Under — back to — horizontal
Outward — from — above
Down — from
Tan clung brown face
Shutting leaned against
So
Knockout
Shoo Shoo
Back standing hand
Advanced slowly
Tentative steps
Cobalt-blue eyes probing.

The Maltese Falcon by Dashiell Hammett,
Chapter 1

Vienna at 2:30 A.M. bites

look like? a room

thinking break

what will I look like

Certainly you your
slight relief

to spend night in wait
exhausted.

at 11:00 A.M. Good

little adjutant wants
morning

4:00 P.M.

just relatively

sends us off

to discuss remaining details
your doing
opposing forces
slowly leave woman and myself
still
How far

An hour But it turns

Jax NTP

**how far is an hour
measured by wants?**

       vienna at 2:30 a.m.   bites
look like   room
thinking   break
what will i look like
certainly you   you
                     slight relief
      spend night   wait
                     exhausted
    11:00 a.m.   good
        little adjutant wants
                   morning
                   1:00 p.m.
             just relatively
    send us off
              discuss   remaining details
                 your doing
         opposing forces
slowly leave   woman and myself
       still
              how far
an hour   but it turns

Letters to Milena by Franz Kafka
Prague, July 5th, 1920: Monday morning

diamonds

her eyes
her mouth

honey.'
me.   cold

silent.

you think   blonde

delight But the loss is
awful people.'
don't know
She gave me a smile

I

came in.
two

and

'I don't know whether I can
go on

Rosemarie Keenan

My Lovely

diamonds
her eyes

her mouth
honey

me
cold
silent

you think blonde
delight
but the loss is awful
people don't know

she gave me a smile
I came in two

and I don't know whether I can go on

Farewell, My Lovely by Raymond Chandler
Chapter 18

quiet
dancers
fall to-
gether

the light
clatter of
turned right angles

battered
darkness.

and
soundlessly,

huge hands
Hard hands, hands with enormous strength
th   a   r

moved, moved like
tortured
eyes.
pressed against
something soft.   something

detached

no longer menacing. No longer important.

Wm. Todd King

Accidental Friends

Quiet dancers
fall together,
the light clatter of turned right angles,
battered darkness,
and soundlessly huge hands,
hard hands,
hands with enormous strength
that moved,
moved like tortured eyes
pressed against something soft,
something detached,
no longer menacing,
no longer important.

"Pick-Up on Noon Street" by Raymond Chandler

She   hollow-cheeked
                                   rocking

gin   smiling.

                                              eyes

                        moving

                to
                      maul him
                       me

Joseph Lisowski

Untitled

hollow-cheeked
rocking gin
smiling eyes
moving
to maul him
me

Red Harvest by Dashiell Hammett
Chapter 10

voices r sharp

how erratic

bitter and icy

what a sick, world.
crazy, crazy, crazy.

voices keep me here

Renee Mallett

Voices

Voices sharp
How erratic
Bitter and icy
What a sick world
Crazy, crazy, crazy.
Their voices keep me here.

Darkness, Take my Hand by Dennis Lehane
Prologue

It was all or nothing ▮▮▮▮ h
▮▮▮.

▮▮▮s one of those rare moments ▮▮▮▮▮▮▮▮▮▮▮n
▮▮▮▮▮▮. ▮▮▮▮▮▮▮ never ▮▮ closer; our hearts,
▮▮▮▮▮▮▮▮▮ never▮▮ more honest.

▮▮▮▮▮▮▮ break down the decades ▮▮▮▮▮t
▮▮▮▮▮▮▮. ▮▮▮▮▮▮▮▮▮▮▮▮t
▮▮ rouse from this feeling. ▮▮▮▮▮▮▮▮▮▮
▮▮▮read the portents and signs.

▮▮▮▮▮▮▮▮▮▮▮▮▮▮v
▮▮▮▮▮▮▮▮▮▮▮▮w
▮▮▮▮▮▮▮."

▮▮blue eyes, ▮▮▮▮▮▮ omniscient▮▮▮▮s
▮▮▮▮▮▮▮▮▮▮▮ thought
and hesitation. ▮▮▮▮▮f my breathing and ▮▮▮▮▮
▮▮ that gaze.

▮▮▮▮▮▮ trying to make it work, ▮▮▮.
▮▮▮▮▮f this special torture, ▮▮▮▮▮
▮▮▮▮▮.

Adrian Manning

It Was All or Nothing

one of those rare moments,
never closer; our hearts never more honest.

break down the decades, rouse from this feeling
read the portents and signs.

blue eyes, omniscient, thought and hesitation,
my breathing and that gaze.

trying to make it work,
this special
torture.

The Long Fall by Walter Mosley
Chapter 42

She was heaving with ███████████████████████

██████████ passion and ████████████████████████
████████████ earrings ███████████████████████████
██
██
██
██
██████████████████████ like someone spearing sal-
mon ███████████████ midstream.
   It was ██████████████████████████████████████
██████████████████████ a lady ████████████████████
██
██████ and she rose accordingly ████████████████████
██
██████████████████████████████████ A blanket order,
both way.
   "Yes, ma'am?" ███████████████████████████████
██████████████████
   The lady ███████████████████████████████████████
smiled. ███
██
██████████████ I became a little confused. ████████
██████████████████████████ like a Venetian gon-
dolier ██.
███████████████ She advanced ██████████████████████
██
██████████████████████████ and ████████████████████
██
███████████████ wriggled almost ecstatically ████████
████████████████████.

Karen Margolis

Yes she smiled

She was heaving
with passion and earrings
like someone spearing
salmon midstream

It was a lady
and she rose accordingly.
A blanket order,
both way.

"Yes, ma'am?"
The lady smiled.
(Yes, the lady smiled.)

I became a little confused
like a Venetian gondolier.
She advanced and wriggled
almost ecstatically.

It was a lady
and she rose accordingly.
A blanket order,
both way.

"Yes, ma'am?"
The lady smiled.
(Yes, the lady smiled)

The Bride Wore Black by Cornell Woolrich
Part Two, Chapter One

DEVIL

stared at me with
dead eyes

a gangster   got   to
smile   hijack   liquor
and cigarettes, sell 'em all over   California
Bad   with a knife
see him
kill
a   loudmouth
dude
eyes came to life   a moment

man
was ready
for a
second

woman
walked up

eyes widened
as if to say
fool   deserve t'be dead
knife appeared
man crumpled

I
laughed softly.

CATFISH MCDARIS

The Devil Lives in California

Devil stared at me with
dead eyes, a gangster got
to smile, hijack liquor
and cigarettes, sell 'em
all over California

Bad with a knife, see him
kill a loudmouth dude, eyes
came to life a moment, man
was ready for a second

Woman walked up, eyes
widened as if to say, fool
deserve t' be dead, knife
appeared, man crumpled

I laughed softly.

Devil in a Blue Dress by Walter Mosley
Chapter 8

turned back, and smiled
"Talk to me,

She   considered me
                                            sure I was

piranha

she'd talk

                                            because she

must
    She

nodded and

watched me with   cold,
eyes,

                        and wondered where this was
going.

Marcia Meara

Piranha

I turned back,
and smiled
Talk to me.
She considered me,
sure I was a piranha.
She'd talk because she must.
She nodded and
watched me with cold eyes,
and wondered
where this was going.

Hell to Pay by Simon R. Green
Chapter 6

a crow   will

Fall

a crow

that's   going to fall

the eyes   the flicker

crazy

a thing in my life

crazy,

a thing in your life

it's

O.K.

O.K.

O.K.

I

I

I

would still

light the fire

64

james w. moore

the crow

a crow will
Fall

a crow
a crow
that's going to fall

the eyes   the flicker

crazy
a thing in my life
crazy
a thing in your life

it's
O.K.
O.K.
O.K.

I

    I

       I

     would still
   light the fire

Double Indemnity by James M. Cain
Chapter 2

I didn't know what to do with my face.
I was hard
illicit bedrooms; informer
to jealousy,

The face
had seen too many   rundown hotel
post-
too many nerve ends showing
the face

You don't want to get
mixed up with me,
had a long journey down from
suffering,
and the other things she had learned

Sarah Nichols

The Mirror

I didn't know what to do with my face. I
was hard
illicit bedrooms,

informer to jealousy.

The face
had seen
too many
rundown hotel postmortems,

too many nerve ends showing.

The face had a long journey
down
from suffering

and
the other things

she had learned.

You don't want to get mixed up with me.

The Moving Target by Ross Macdonald
Chapter 8

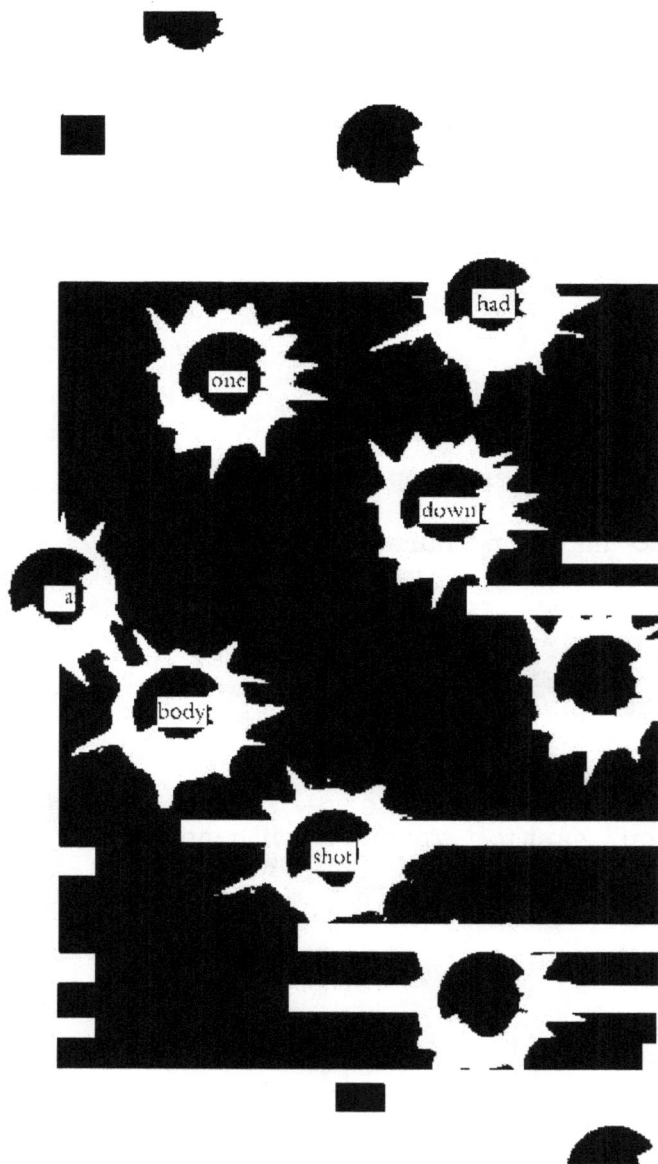

had

one

down

a

body

shot

Winston Plowes

Bullets

had

one
 down

A
 body
  shot

The Thin Man by Dashiell Hammett
Chapter 15

financing ████████████ distribution deal, ████████
██
████████████████████ make the movie. ████████
████████████████ hands-on. ████ Erin—the work is hard. Long
hours, lotta retakes, ████████████████████████████
██
██
████████████
██
████████████████████████████ a set of kneepads ████
██
████████████████ for getting the job."
    "Exactly," ████████████ "You understand the business."
    "Oh hooray," ████████████████████████████████
████████
████████████████████████████████████
████ know her," ████████. ████████████████████
████████ know any guys named Misty?" ████.
████████████
████████████ know ████████████████
    "Melissa ████
    "Never heard of her. She must ████████████████
████████████████████████████ 't need a ████████
████████████████████████ "
████████████████████████████████████
████████████████ career, ████████ How did she spend
her days."
    "Working out, as far as I know."
    "That's all?"

David S. Pointer

Financing   distribution deal
     make the movie
Hands-on. Erin—the work is hard.
Long hours, lotta retakes.

     set of kneepads

for getting the job.

"Exactly." "You understand the business."

"Oh hooray."

     know
Know any guys named Misty?
     know
Melissa?
     Never heard of her
       She must
    need a
career, How did she spend her days
Working out,
"That's all?"

Blue Screen by Robert B. Parker
Chapter 16

Two or three cars flicked by in the crisp fall night, but the sidewalks were dark and empty.

Pete ▮▮▮▮▮ he saw the girl again.

She was pressed against a wall, motionless. Faint light from somewhere touched one side of her face. He knew it was the same girl.

He stepped into a doorway, watched her.

Lights stabbed into the street from the corner behind

Pete ▮▮▮▮▮ e stiffened at the sharp sound of running steps, clicking high heels.

The girl was running toward him along the sidewalk Pete stepped out of the doorway, grabbed her arm, dragged her back into the doorway.

The girl panted at his side.

"I can't do it. I'm scared," the girl gasped in Pete ▮▮▮ s ear. Then she broke away from him

D.A. Pratt

Escape

Two or three cars flicked by
in the crisp fall night,
but the sidewalks were dark and empty.
Pete saw the girl again.
She was pressed against a wall, motionless.
Faint light from somewhere touched
one side of her face.
He knew it was the same girl.
He stepped into a doorway, watched her.
Lights stabbed into the street
from the corner behind.
Pete stiffened at the sharp sound
of running steps, clicking high heels.
The girl was running toward him
along the sidewalk.
Pete stepped out of the doorway,
grabbed her arm, dragged her back
into the doorway. The girl panted at his side.
"I can't do it. I'm scared," the girl gasped
in Pete's ear. Then she broke away
from him.

"Pick Up on Noon Street" by Raymond Chandler

grab

count

swarm scream

slice

quickly

run

twist yank

pant knife

stitch

and then

turn

close

reach

close no light

go

sit

tell feel

74

David Rachels

Hell's Our Destination 85

grab count
swarm scream
slice quickly
run twist yank
pant knife stitch

and then

turn close
reach close

no light

go
sit
tell
feel

Hell's Our Destination by Gil Brewer, page 85
Reprinted by permission of Marvin N. Lee

I got nothing ▆▆▆▆▆▆▆▆▆▆▆▆▆
got wise. ▆▆ wise ▆▆▆▆▆▆▆▆▆▆▆▆▆▆▆▆
smile ▆▆▆▆▆, like a crooked Santa Claus mask, ▆▆
battered ▆▆

▆▆▆▆▆▆▆▆▆▆▆▆▆▆▆▆▆▆▆▆▆▆
▆▆▆▆▆▆▆▆▆▆▆▆▆▆▆ but strong and fast, ▆▆

▆▆▆▆▆▆▆▆▆▆▆▆▆▆▆ expressive, ▆▆

large hands ▆▆▆▆▆▆▆▆▆▆▆▆▆

▆▆▆▆▆▆▆▆▆

▆▆▆▆▆▆▆▆▆ laborious ▆▆▆▆▆▆▆▆▆▆▆
▆▆▆▆▆ "
" ▆▆▆▆▆▆▆▆▆▆▆▆▆▆▆▆

▆▆▆▆▆▆▆▆▆▆▆▆▆▆▆▆▆▆▆▆▆▆▆▆
▆▆▆▆▆▆▆▆▆▆▆▆▆▆▆▆▆▆▆▆▆▆▆▆

▆▆▆▆ ."

▆▆▆▆▆▆▆ air issued from his mouth and nostrils ▆▆
▆ body-punched ▆▆
▆▆▆▆▆▆▆▆▆▆▆▆▆▆ to keep his fifty points .
of I.Q. occupied.
▆ got ▆▆▆▆▆▆ nothing to do ▆▆▆▆▆
▆▆ over the Nevada line. He ▆▆▆▆▆▆▆▆▆
▆▆ came ▆▆▆▆▆▆▆
▆▆▆▆▆▆▆▆ with the terrible effort of ▆▆▆ .

▆▆▆▆▆▆▆▆▆▆▆▆▆▆▆▆▆▆▆▆▆▆▆▆
▆▆▆▆▆▆▆▆▆▆▆ "
▆▆▆▆▆▆▆ the concrete block ▆▆▆▆▆▆▆▆
▆▆▆▆▆▆▆▆▆▆ "

Jonne Rhodes

Bully

I got nothing
got wise.
wise smile
like a crooked Santa Claus mask,
battered but strong and fast,
expressive, large hands laborious
air issued from his mouth and nostrils
body-punched
to keep his fifty
points of I.Q. occupied.
got nothing to do
over the Nevada line.
He came with the terrible
effort of the concrete block

The Drowning Pool by Ross Macdonald
Chapter 14

Rembrandt on the calendar that year,
smeary self-portrait ▮ imperfectly
▮ smeared palette
dirty thumb ▮

▮ His face
▮ full of the disgust of life ▮

four-thirty ▮ the phone rang ▮

'You are Philip Marlowe, a private detective?'

▮ a man who can be trusted to keep his mouth
shut. ▮

▮ I live at 4212 Cabrillo Street,
Montemar Vista. Do you know where that is?'
'I know where Montemar Vista is, Mr Marriott.'

Van Roberts

Montemar Vista

              Rembrandt on the calendar that year,
smeary self-portrait   imperfectly
                        smeared palette
dirty thumb

                              His face
          full of the disgust of life

four-thirty   the phone rang

'You are Philip Marlowe, a private detective?'

        a man who can be trusted to keep his mouth
shut.

        I live at 4212 Cabrillo Street,
Montemar Vista. Do you know where that is?
        'I know where Montemar Vista is, Mr Marriott.'

Farewell My Lovely by Raymond Chandler
Chapter 7

Daniel Romo

to clear the traffic
where bodies
weld into
art
watch 'em
start
to
crash

The Zero by Jess Walter
Part Two

81

At one o'clock ▓▓▓▓▓▓▓▓▓▓▓ the night ▓▓▓▓ turned
down ▓▓▓▓▓▓▓▓▓▓▓▓▓▓▓▓▓▓▓▓▓▓▓▓▓▓▓▓▓▓▓▓▓▓
▓▓▓▓▓▓▓▓▓ The blue ◀▓▓▓ darkened shade ▓▓▓
▓▓▓▓▓▓drew back ▓▓▓▓▓▓▓▓▓▓▓▓▓▓▓▓▓▓▓▓▓
shadowy ▓▓▓▓▓▓▓▓▓ córners ▓▓ memories like cobwebs.
▓▓▓▓▓▓▓▓▓▓▓▓▓▓▓▓▓▓▓▓▓▓▓▓▓▓▓▓▓▓▓▓▓▓▓
▓▓▓▓▓▓▓▓▓▓▓▓▓▓▓▓▓▓▓▓▓▓▓▓▓▓▓▓▓▓▓▓▓▓▓

▓▓▓▓▓▓▓▓▓▓▓ after one A.M. ▓▓▓▓▓▓▓▓▓▓▓▓▓▓
▓▓▓▓▓▓▓▓▓▓▓▓▓▓▓▓▓▓▓▓▓▓▓▓▓▓▓▓
▓▓▓▓▓▓▓▓▓▓▓▓▓▓▓▓▓▓▓▓▓▓▓▓ quirked at the
corners ▓▓▓▓▓▓▓▓▓▓▓▓▓▓▓▓▓▓▓▓▓▓▓▓▓▓▓▓▓▓▓
▓▓▓▓▓▓▓▓▓▓▓▓▓▓▓▓▓▓▓▓ clasped ▓▓▓▓▓▓▓▓
▓▓▓▓▓▓▓▓▓▓▓▓▓▓▓▓▓▓▓▓▓▓▓▓▓▓▓▓▓▓▓▓▓▓▓
▓▓▓▓▓▓▓▓▓▓▓▓▓▓▓▓▓▓▓▓ at the ends. ▓▓▓▓▓▓▓
▓▓▓▓▓▓▓▓▓▓▓▓▓▓▓▓▓▓▓▓▓▓▓▓▓▓▓ and there
was peace in ▓▓ quiet sea-gray ▓▓▓
▓▓▓▓▓▓▓▓▓▓▓▓▓▓▓▓▓▓▓▓▓▓▓▓▓▓▓▓▓▓▓▓▓▓▓
▓▓▓▓▓ leaning back ▓▓▓▓▓▓▓▓▓▓▓▓▓▓▓▓▓▓▓▓▓▓▓
balanced ▓▓▓▓▓▓ perfectly still, ▓▓▓▓▓▓▓▓▓▓▓
.

Tere Sievers

Waiting

At one o'clock
the night turned down
the blue darkened shade
drew back shadowy corners,
memories like cobwebs.
After one a.m.
quirked at the corners
clasped at the ends
there was peace
in quiet, sea-grey
leaning back, balanced
perfectly still.

"I'll Be Waiting" by Raymond Chandler

Victorian whorehouse   an

                          ornate figure

drapes   the long window

                     black leather with brass

studs

red   spill

trickled down onto   white brick sill.

84

Gerald So

Victorian Whorehouse

An ornate figure
drapes the long window

in black leather with brass studs,
red spill

trickled down onto
white brick sill.

The *Godwulf Manuscript* by Robert B. Parker
Chapter 1

York New

Christ, Washington himself

to Mary and

ramifications

The

goddamn

orders from

"Yes.

I believe

you know.

is

for

him

to derail

whereabouts

envisioned he

can

wrong

her

Naturally, talk

was of

coffee

a large

Sherry Steiner

New York
Washington
Christ
himself to
Mary and
ramifications—
The goddamn orders from
yes
I believe you know
is
for
him—
To derail
whereabouts
envisioned
he can
wrong her—
Naturally,
talk was
of coffee
a large—

Murder at Union Station by Margaret Truman
Chapter 42

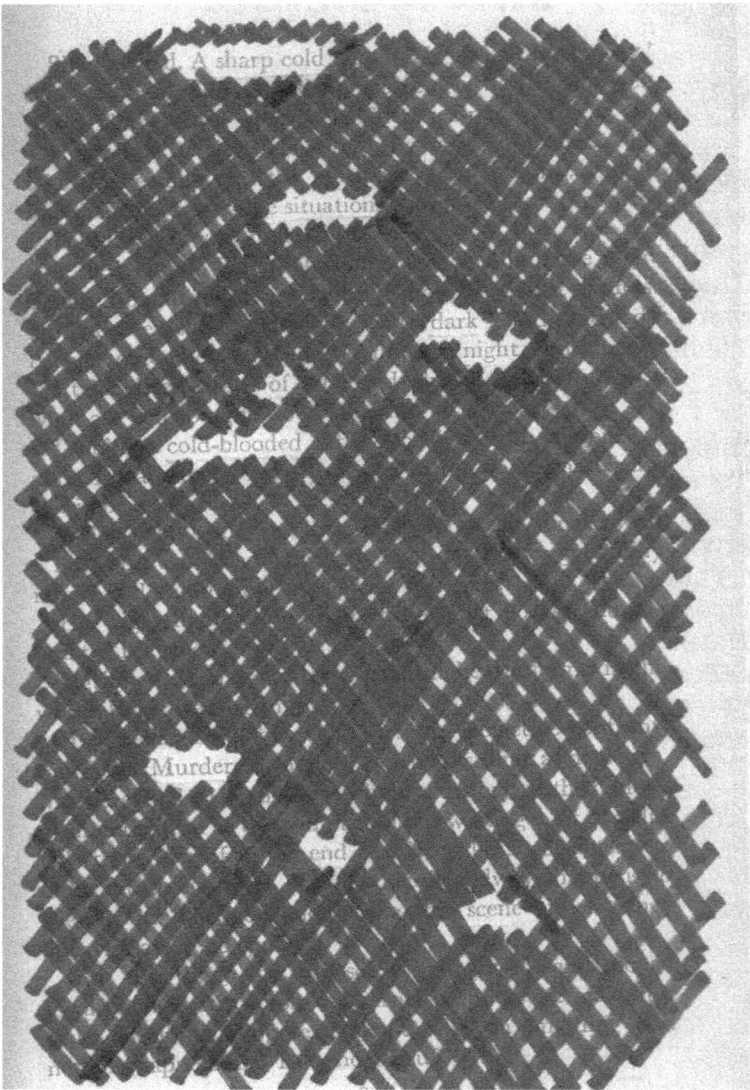

A sharp cold

situation

dark
night

of
cold-blooded

Murder

end

scene

Caitlin Stern

Finale

A sharp cold situation
dark night
of cold-blooded murder
End scene

The Lady in the Lake by Raymond Chandler
Chapter 31

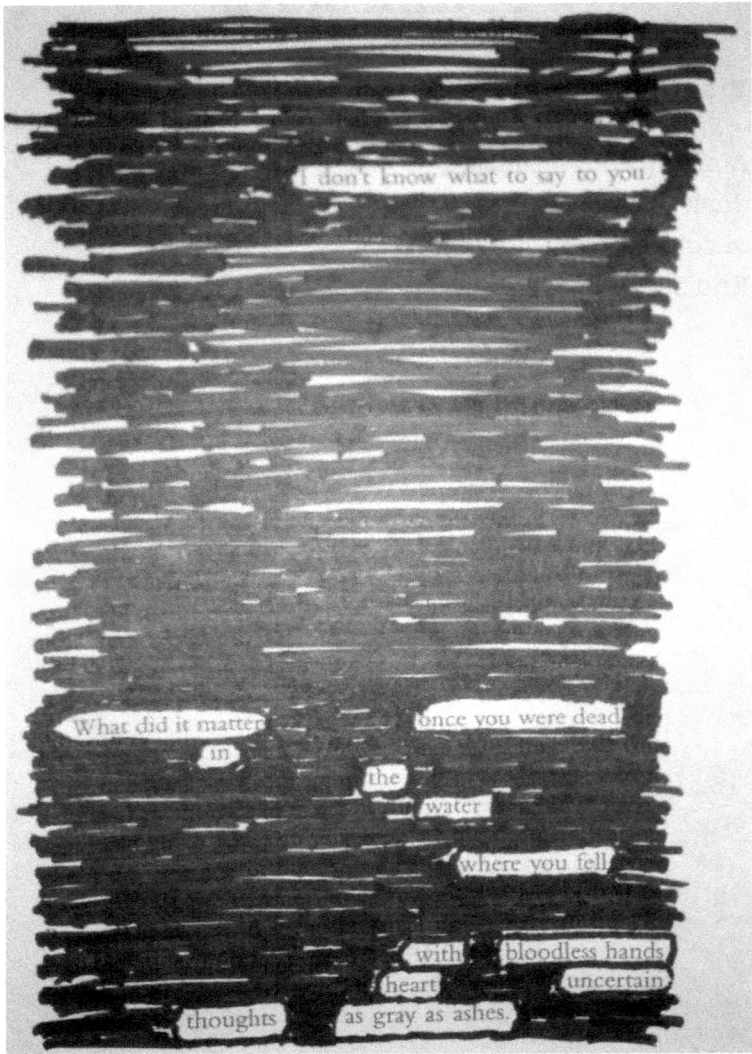

I don't know what to say to you.

What did it matter
in
the
water
where you fell
once you were dead

with bloodless hands
heart uncertain
thoughts as gray as ashes.

90

Scott Stoller

Untitled

I don't know what
to say to you.

What did it matter once you were
dead in the water

where you fell with
bloodless hands

heart uncertain
thoughts as gray as ashes.

The Big Sleep by Raymond Chandler
Chapter 32

"[blacked out] a mistake," I said. [blacked out] didn't want to see [blacked out]

He inclined his silver head and said politely: [blacked out] many mistakes." He closed the door against [blacked out]

I stood [blacked out] breathing [blacked out] winding [blacked out] Beyond the [blacked out] miles. [blacked out]

I walked [blacked out] the [blacked out] air [blacked out] started downtown."

She had lovely legs [blacked out] smooth [blacked out] *Rare* [blacked out] up finding out.

[blacked out]

Thomas R. Thomas

I stood breathing

I stood breathing
Winding
Beyond the miles.

I walked
the
air.

She had lovely legs
Smooth
Rare

and

I wait

back to the sunpainted
awake to the morning excitement
the breeze tickling her cheek
the semblance of gems
paused expectantly
d from slumber to clear-eyed liveliness
the unfamiliar fragrance
the smooth precision of a globe revolving on a fixed axis
Sighing puffs of breath
opaquely glistening eyes
enamelled shoes.

Mary Umans

from slumber to clear-eyed liveliness
her back to the sunpainted wall
awake to the morning excitement
the breeze tickling her cheek
the smooth precision of a globe
revolving on a fixed axis,
Signing puffs of breath
The semblance of gems
Opaquely glistening eyes
And enameled shoes.
Paused expectantly.

"The Ruffian's Wife" by Dashiell Hammett

THE ATMOSPHERE became stranger the days went on. something had gone the realness broad daylight thousands of honking human voices left the pier

before on water on deck he had drowned something he could remember how to swim water below him, miles deep have to look at it he felt

Melanie Villines

Miles Deep

The atmosphere
became stranger
the days went on
something had gone
the realness
in broad daylight
thousands of honking
human voices
left the pier

before on water
on deck
he had drowned something
he could remember
how to swim
water below him, miles deep
have to look at it
most of the time
he felt

The Talented Mr. Ripley by Patricia Highsmith
Chapter 4

another you.
last month. again.
another city for you."
blue
Cramped.
ironic "Now what
papers
say talk turned frowned dark-faced man.
Through with rough -faced
boys finished with the girl."
the closed door knocked
On
Come in."
open follow into
Silver a big black
and white bed
The girl facing
eighteen wore gray

Mercedes Webb-Pullman

another you

last month
again another city
blue, cramped

ironic now
what papers say
talk turn frown

dark-faced man
through with
rough faced boys

finished with the girl
the closed door
knocked on

come, open and follow
into silver
a big black and white bed

the girl facing eighteen
wore gray

"A Man Called Spade" by Dashiell Hammett

I am nearly at the end now.

there were many difficulties, many dramas, but I do
not   belong to the story I am trying to tell.
                                        I lived apart for almost a year.
                              there were months of confusion
                                    From the vantage point of this
                              the only thing that matters.
the facts of my life are purely incidental.
On 23 February 1981,

                              we moved across the river,

                                                        In September,
                        We all went to Minnesota
and by the time we got back,

                                        I never talked about him.
                                said nothing,

                                    and officially stopped writing

          we decided to live together again,   in
strictly practical terms.

                                                    As a final step,

Richard Wink

I am nearly at the end now
There were many difficulties, many dramas, but I do
Not belong to the story I am trying to tell.
I lived apart for almost a year.
There were months of confusion
From the vantage point of this
The only thing that matters
The facts of my life are purely incidental.
On 23 February 1981,
We moved across the river,
In September
We all went to Minnesota
And by the time we got back,
I never talked about him
Said nothing
And officially stopped writing
We decided to live together again, in
Strictly practical terms.
As a final step

The New York Trilogy by Paul Auster
Part III, Chapter 9

swiftly ▮▮▮▮▮ frightened eyes, ▮▮▮▮▮
not raise her ▮▮▮▮▮▮▮▮ nothing
▮▮▮s face ▮▮▮▮▮ he ▮▮ noticed ▮▮▮▮▮s
fright, turned ▮▮▮▮▮▮▮▮ and called ▮ his
hoarse ▮▮▮▮▮fact voice. ▮▮▮▮▮
▮▮▮▮▮ a spotted Great Dane ▮▮▮▮,
▮▮▮▮▮ in dinner clothes, ▮▮▮▮
walked straight to ▮▮▮▮▮ nuzzled her hand. She
▮▮▮▮▮ two men ▮▮▮▮ entered. There
was no timidity, ▮▮▮▮▮ in her ▮▮
▮▮▮▮▮ a gray
tweed, ▮▮▮▮▮ topcoat—▮ came to her, smiling.
▮▮▮▮▮ where you landed ▮▮▮▮ vanished as ▮
▮▮▮▮▮ the bandages, ▮▮▮▮
perhaps forty years old, ▮▮▮▮▮, graceful ▮▮▮▮
▮▮▮ with ▮▮▮▮▮
▮▮▮▮▮ a close-clipped dark mustache.
▮ pushed the dog aside and took the woman ▮▮▮.
"It is not serious, ▮▮▮▮." She did not smile. Her
voice ▮▮▮▮▮ stumbled in the ▮▮▮▮ twisted ▮▮
ankle. ▮▮▮▮▮
He turned to the man ▮▮▮▮▮
▮▮▮▮▮ briskly: "Thanks ever so much ▮▮▮▮
▮▮▮▮▮ aren't you?"
▮▮▮▮ the sweater nodded. ▮▮▮▮

"Right." ▮▮▮▮▮
▮▮▮▮▮

Joanie Hieger Fritz Zosike

Swiftly frightened eyes not raise her nothing face.
He noticed fright, turned and called his hoarse fact voice.
A spotted Great Dane in dinner clothes walked straight
To nuzzle her hand. She two men entered. There was
No timidity in her.

A gray tweed topcoat...came to her, smiling.
Where you landed vanished as the bandages,
Perhaps forty years old, graceful with a close
Clipped dark mustache pushed the dog aside
And took the woman.

"It is not serious." She did not smile. Her voice
Stumbled in the twisted ankle.
He turned to the man briskly:
"Thanks ever so much, aren't you?"
The sweater nodded: "Right."

Woman in the Dark, Dashiell Hammett
Chapter One

Notes from the Poets

BETH AYER: Writing erasure poetry from noir fiction was an interesting experience as someone not very familiar with the genre. I found that the repetition of certain words and word patterns on a single page (that seems common to noir prose) lent itself naturally to found poetry.

DAVID BARKER: I selected this author because I've always loved Raymond Chandler's prose. His language is rich and colorful. It's incredibly poetic for what was considered at the time to be simply cheap pulp trash fiction. He was a master. I used this particular book because it's one of the few I have on hand, and I love the stories. The way I have gone about making erasure poems (something new to me before this project) is to read through the book quickly, marking pages with phrases or single words that catch my attention because they seem like good material for a poem. I photocopy these pages and then read them again more carefully, circling the parts that originally caught my eye. From there, I start looking for other bits of text before and after these circled parts that expand the selected words into some sort of a narrative. The trick is to not be overpowered by the original narrative as written by the author. I've learned that the texts are almost holographic, in that parts selected at random still hold portions of the original meaning and feel of the source text. Even if you take only a small percentage of the available words, a surprising amount of the original content comes across. I had to consciously work at "breaking" the original meaning by selecting unlikely words that form a new narrative that is not derivative of the source text. I think of erasure poems as being like a word game where there are an infinite number of possible answers, all of them correct. Crafting an original work from the raw material of an existing work makes this a more legitimate form of literature than the casual reader might suspect. It's far beyond mere "found poetry," because creative decisions are made at every step. Once all the words are selected, erasing the unwanted parts of the text was just play for me—having fun with paint and ink. The most I could hope for from that step was to use color and form to group the words into related chunks of narrative, to help make the meaning clearer.

KIM COOPER: I am a great admirer of James M. Cain's dyspeptic portrait of Southern California. This hardbound edition of *Postman* provided the model for the typography and layout of my own mystery novel *The Kept Girl*, so it was natural to open it up when asked to create a noir erasure poem. Any page in this brutal narrative of unchecked desire and relentless fate could spark a poem. I picked 29, in honor of the year in which *The Kept Girl* is set. Some very bad things happen on page 29—prematurely bad things punctuated with frenzied attempts to set them right. I blacked all the specifics out, leaving just a few nightmarish words meant to evoke the heavy horror of responsibility that accompanies evil action.

ANDREA JANELLE DICKENS: A challenge I always face in found poetry is how well I know the story. I like being unfamiliar with the works I use as sources, so that the poem becomes a meeting of my own poetic voice with the voice of the author of the source text. It had been decades since I'd thought about *The Maltese Falcon*. I thought that would be to my advantage. And yet, page after page of working on poems from this novel, I found myself facing the very strong voice of Dashiell Hammett. It took a while to find my own voice able to stand up alongside his. That challenge was the joy of playing around with this writing prompt.

CHRIS FORHAN: I liked finding an inward, whispery lyric "I"—a voice that sounds candid with yearning—within Chandler's outward-looking prose, with its plot movements and conversations between characters who reveal themselves only partially and grudgingly. Once I discovered, or uncovered, the statement "I wanted / the / hundred lonely / things," I was off and running: I felt a generating impulse for whatever might follow, and I let that impulse govern my subsequent choices for what to erase, what to save.

Although an exercise in erasure presents me, by chance, with language to make use of, it is not unlike the writing of any poem. In listening to language, whether it is given to me by another text or by my own pen, I try to leave myself open to the implications that are already in the language, to the direction in which it wants to go; in other words, I want to be continually surprised. In writing the poem, I want to move away from intention and toward meaningful mystery. The finished poem, then, if it is a poem, should feel unerringly true but also slightly beyond my understanding. Its accelerations, leaps, and swerves should lead it to land, ultimately, perhaps a little off balance, gesturing toward some next, unspoken thing, whatever that might be.

DEBORAH HERMAN: I fully intended to create found poetry out of Dashiell Hammett's *The Thin Man* with little regard for the plot being laid out on the page, but I found with hardboiled fiction that the writing was so terse that there really were very few adjectives to work with or cull from. So, instead, I undermined the agency of the male leads. I changed the voice so that a "dame," "skirt," or hooker was speaking in the confessional mode.

KAREN MARGOLIS: Erasure poetry—fine. Noir?—well, not so easy if you happen to live in Berlin, Germany, a city where classic genre twentieth-century books in English aren't exactly paving the sidewalks.

A quick Internet search came up with predictable hits for Chandler, Hammett, and their kind. Meanwhile I was hooked on the theme and started following up all kinds of clues . . . until finally a reference to the landmark Truffaut noir film from 1968 led me to the author William Irish—alias Cornell Woolrich—and his great noir novel from 1940, *The Bride Wore Black*. Now I simply had to get hold of the book. In the whole of Berlin there was only one copy to be had. My inquiries took me on a rainy July day to a big secondhand book dealer in a backyard in the city's Kreuzberg district. The damp musty smell of old books stacked to the ceiling matched the weather. The man at the counter looked at me gloomily, but the moment I said the title his eyes lit up and he reached back to the shelf behind him. "A rare find," he said, handing me the book. "The 1984 Ballantine pocket edition! You're a lucky woman!"

I paid the modest price quickly and left before he decided it was worth more. The book was in pretty good shape—the cover with its dramatic shadowy illustration intact, and the inside pages yellowed but with very few age spots.

Reading the story, then choosing the page for erasure, I felt like a lucky woman indeed. The bride wore black when she took her revenge. I wielded a black felt pen to give the page a new meaning. This erasure adventure was a perfect literary empowerment. (Berlin, November 2013)

MARCIA MEARA: I love Simon R. Green's *Tales From the Nightside*. All of the books, including *Hell To Pay*, combine dangerously creepy urban fantasy with dark noir concepts that appeal to my sense of humor. After all, nothing says noir like a trench coat and a private eye, even if the private eye is actually an invisible modified organ that excels at finding lost things. When I pulled out the words for "Piranha," I was using my own private eye to see a woman, wary of a man who might or might not be in a position of authority over her. She thinks of him as a piranha—a danger to her—and only talks to him because she knows she has no choice.

JAMES W. MOORE: my experience creating the poem was largely influenced by the title. as i started to look for a poem on the pages of Cain's terse, wonderfully grotesque work, i kept finding mirror images and reflections of text, doubles everywhere. i began by hacking away anything wasn't repeated. then i backed up and dug out the connecting tissue to make those doubles a poem, like reassembling a crime scene.

SARAH NICHOLS: I chose Ross Macdonald's novel because I love his language. All of these different Californias are evoked and filtered through the conscious of Lew Archer, so they can't help but become noir. The erasure poem, my first, was an exercise in patience, as I would continually cross out words that I wanted to use. The poem took shape, and came to life.

D.A. PRATT: When Catfish McDaris first encouraged me to consider creating an erasure poem for this anthology, my own mini-collection of what might be considered "noir fiction" was packed away. Therefore I had to resort to what was available at the Regina Public Library. In my search for something "noir," I developed the impression that library collections, now increasingly subjected to being culled from time to time, may be losing touch with the works that are traditionally considered "noir." Parenthetically, this is an ongoing danger in many areas of public libraries. Nevertheless, I was content to encounter a collection of shorter works by Raymond Chandler with which to work. I will note that I was definitely looking to create an erasure poem about a woman. With this in mind, I actually almost turned to the trilogy featuring Lisbeth Salander, a really great female character, since one source I consulted about what qualified as "noir" mentioned *The Girl With the Dragon Tattoo*... but I didn't—my copies of that trilogy were also packed away at the time. And I was happy to look at what Raymond Chandler had to offer, even though I personally wonder if he's essentially "hardboiled" more than "noir." The real challenge for me is the fact that my "poetic style," if I indeed have one, is much more narrative than erasure poems probably are going to end up being. My effort in this anthology is my first ever erasure poem, and I would like to thank the editor for her initial comments, which very much improved the poem as presented.

DAVID RACHELS: At PulpFest 2012, I purchased an original copy of Gil Brewer's classic noir *Hell's Our Destination* for a dollar. Later, when I later examined the book closely, I discovered that some of its pages were missing—so I disassembled the book and made some poems.

JONNE RHODES: I looked for masters of noir fiction writing, since I knew little about the genre. Ross Macdonald and Dashiell Hammett were among the best. I read pages of their work, until words appeared in an order that was quirky and dark. It was like mining for gold. Outbursts of fool's gold laughter and "Eureka!" moments punctuated this prospector's search. Macdonald describes the character on page one hundred twenty six with "a carnival clown eeriness, grounded with the weight of a bully." I hoped to preserve that strange mixture in the erasure poem.

SHERRY STEINER: I have a ton of discarded paperbacks that I use to recreate. I found *Murder at Union Station* in the pile, whereby I randomly flipped to a page and it opened to 309!

CAITLIN STERN: The first thing I did was rummage through the bookshelves for appropriate noir books. I found several good options, and flipped through the pages of each one, waiting for a word to catch my eye. One such word was "murderer," which I built "Finale" around, eventually shortening the word to "murder." I underlined every word with a similar tone, and hunted for words to string them together, erasing anything that didn't quite fit.

SCOTT STOLLER: I have a thing for film noir, and love Bogart and Bacall in *The Big Sleep,* which is why I chose that novel to work with. Erasure poems are a game, a puzzle to solve, and it's fun to turn text written by someone else into something with a different feel and meaning. My better ones come together quickly, and start from a particular phrase jumping out at me from the page. I try to keep them spare and short and use as little of the existing text as possible.

MELANIE VILLINES: While editing the Silver Birch Press *Noir Erasure Poetry Anthology*, I realized that only one poem originated from fiction by a woman author—Sherry Steiner's, based on a page from the Margaret Truman mystery novel *Murder at Union Station*. While Truman isn't associated with noir or hardboiled fiction, I decided that she was close enough—and was glad to add a woman author to the mix. This inspired me to base my own poem on the work of a female writer—and it wasn't a stretch because Patricia Highsmith is one of my favorite authors. From the first word, her stories just flow, flow, flow. I've tried to figure out how she achieves her effects, but get so caught up in the story and characters that I forget to analyze her craft. For my erasure poem, I selected a page that started with the words "the atmosphere"—because atmosphere is everything in noir fiction.

About the Authors

PAUL AUSTER is an author and director whose writing blends absurdism, existentialism, crime fiction, and the search for identity and personal meaning in works such as *The New York Trilogy* (1987), *Moon Palace* (1989), *The Music of Chance* (1990), *The Book of Illusions* (2002), and *The Brooklyn Follies* (2005).

GIL BREWER (1922-1983) published dozens of novels and more than a hundred stories under his own name and a variety of pseudonyms. His bestselling novel, *13 French Street*, was published in 1951 and sold over a million copies.

CHARLES BUKOWSKI (1920-1994) was a poet, novelist, and short story writer who wrote thousands of poems, hundreds of short stories, and six novels, including the hardboiled *Pulp* (1994).

JAMES M. CAIN (1892-1977) was an author and journalist associated with the hardboiled school of American crime writing and considered a pioneer of noir fiction. Cain's first novel, *The Postman Always Rings Twice*, was published in 1934. Two years later, his novella, *Double Indemnity*, was serialized in *Liberty* magazine.

RAYMOND CHANDLER (1888-1959) is considered a founder of the hardboiled school of detective fiction. His first short story, "Blackmailers Don't Shoot," was published in *Black Mask* during 1933, and his first novel, *The Big Sleep*, was published in 1939. Chandler's seven novels include: *Farewell, My Lovely* (1940), *The Little Sister* (1949), and *The Long Goodbye* (1953).

SIMON R. GREEN is a science fiction and fantasy author whose works include the bestselling *Deathstalker* cycle, the *New York Times* bestseller *Robin Hood: Prince of Thieves*, and many other novels. His writing explores the opposition of light and dark forces that characterizes noir.

DASHIELL HAMMETT (1894-1961) wrote detective novels, short stories, and screenplays. He created a variety of enduring characters, including Sam Spade (*The Maltese Falcon*), Nick and Nora Charles (*The Thin Man*), and the Continental Op (*Red Harvest* and *The Dain Curse*). *The New York Times* called him "the dean of the...hardboiled school of detective fiction."

110

PATRICIA HIGHSMITH (1921-1995) was known for her psychological thrillers. Her first novel, *Strangers on a Train*, has been adapted for stage and screen numerous times, notably by Alfred Hitchcock in 1951. In addition to her acclaimed series about murderer Tom Ripley, she wrote many short stories.

FRANZ KAFKA (1883-1924), a German-language writer, is considered one of the most influential authors of the twentieth century. His work includes the novels The *Trial* and *The Castle* and the novella *The Metamorphosis*. Many regard him as the father of noir.

DENNIS LEHANE is a Boston-based novelist whose books include *Mystic River* (2001) and *Shutter Island* (2003).

ROSS MACDONALD, the pseudonym of Kenneth Millar (1915-1983), is best known for his series of hardboiled novels set in Southern California featuring private detective Lew Archer.

WALTER MOSLEY has written a series of best-selling historical mysteries featuring Easy Rawlins, an African American private investigator and World War II veteran living in the Watts neighborhood of Los Angeles.

ROBERT B. PARKER (1932-2010) was a crime writer whose novels feature the private detective Spenser.

MARGARET TRUMAN (1924-2008) was a singer who later became the successful author of murder mysteries and a number of historical works, including a biography of her father, President Harry S. Truman.

JESS WALTER is the author of novels, short stories, and works of nonfiction. He is the recipient of the Edgar Allen Poe Award, and was a finalist for the National Book Award in 2006.

CORNELL WOOLRICH (1903-1968) was a novelist and short story writer who sometimes wrote under the pseudonyms William Irish and George Hopley. More film noir screenplays have been adapted from works by Woolrich than any other crime novelist.

About the Poets

JEFF ALFIER is a five-time Pushcart nominee and the author of *The Wolf Yearling* (Silver Birch Press, 2013) and *Idyll for a Vanishing River* (Glass Lyre Press, 2013). He is the founder and co-editor of *San Pedro River Review*.

BETH AYER, based in Providence, Rhode Island, is the Senior Poetry Editor/ Web Manager for the *Found Poetry Review*. In April 2013, she was one of eighty-five poets to create poems from the eighty-five Pulitzer Prize-winning works of fiction as part of the Pulitzer Remix project.

JENNI B. BAKER is the founder and editor-in-chief of *The Found Poetry Review* (foundpoetryreview.com). Her own poetry—both found and not—has been published in more than two dozen literary journals. She currently resides in Bethesda, Maryland. For more information, visit jennibbaker.com.

DAVID BARKER's short stories and poems have been published in many small press chapbooks, little magazines, and anthologies in the U.S. and Europe since the early 1970s. In 2011, Bottle Of Smoke Press published his novel, *Death At The Flea Circus,* and another novel, *Stella Vero,* has been accepted by Bottle of Smoke Press. In 2012-13, he published a serialized horror novel, *Electro-Thrall Zombies*, and in 2013 *Opal's Trails*—a book of poems about nature diarist, Opal Whiteley—was published by Pig Ear Press. David is currently collaborating with W. H. Pugmire on a Lovecraftian horror novella, *The Revenant of Rebecca Pascal,* and with Jordan Hofer on a nonfiction book about alien abductions, *Little Gray Bastards.*

KATHY BURKETT: Kathy Burkett lives in Florida with her husband and two dachshunds. Her writing has been published in various small press publications in print and online, including *Nerve Cowboy, Menacing Hedge,* and *The Red Fez.* She participated in the Pulitzer Remix project in 2013, and dreams of being a professional kazoo player or professional cloud watcher.

CANDACE BUTLER: Candace Butler is an MFA candidate at Antioch University of Los Angeles. She is a writer, artist, and musician residing in her hometown of Sugar Grove, Virginia, a small town in the Appalachian Mountains.

FREDA BUTLER is from southern Virginia in the Appalachian Mountains. She is surrounded by a lovely forest and beautiful wildlife. Her favorite diversions are capturing moments in time via writing and photography, creating recipes for a future cookbook, visiting art museums, listening to music, and traveling.

KIM COOPER is creator of 1947project (1947project.com), the crime-a-day time travel blog that spawned Esotouric's popular crime bus tours, including the Real Black Dahlia (www.esotouric.com). With husband Richard Schave, Kim curates the Salons of LAVA— The Los Angeles Visionaries Association (lavatransforms.org). When the third generation Angeleno isn't combing old newspapers for forgotten scandals, she is a passionate advocate for historic preservation of signage, vernacular architecture, and writers' homes. Kim was for many years the editrix of *Scram*, a journal of unpopular culture. Her books include *Fall in Love for Life, Bubblegum Music Is the Naked Truth, Lost in the Grooves,* and an oral history of the cult band Neutral Milk Hotel. Her latest book is *The Kept Girl* (thekeptgirl.com).

SUBHANKAR DAS is a poet, film producer, bookstore owner, and publisher of Bangla experimental material. He produced six short films that have been honored at international film festivals, and has translated the works Allen Ginsberg and Charles Bukowski into Bangla.

ANDREA JANELLE DICKENS splits her time between Mesa, Arizona, and Oxfordshire, England, and teaches in the Writing Programs at Arizona State University. In her spare time, she is a ceramic artist and beekeeper. Her poems have recently appeared or are forthcoming in *Wayfarer, New South Review, Found Poetry Review,* and *Ruminate.*

BARBARA EKNOIAN's work has appeared in *Pearl, Chiron Review,* Silver Birch Press anthologies, *Re)Verb, New Verse News,* and *Your Daily Poem.* She has been twice nominated for a Pushcart Prize. Her first novel, *Chances Are: A Jersey Girl Comes of Age,* and her poetry book, *Why I Miss New Jersey,* published by Everhart Press, were both recently released and are available at Amazon.com. Her new mantra is Carpe Diem.

CHRIS FORHAN, born and raised in Seattle, Washington, is the author, most recently, of the chapbook *Ransack and Dance* (Silver Birch Press, 2013). His other books include *Black Leapt In*, winner of the Barrow Street Press Poetry Prize; *The Actual Moon, The Actual*

Stars, winner of the Morse Poetry Prize and a Washington State Book Award; and *Forgive Us Our Happiness*, winner of the Bakeless Prize. His poems have appeared in *Poetry, Paris Review, Ploughshares, New England Review, Parnassus*, and other magazines, as well as in *The Best American Poetry*. He has won a National Endowment for the Arts Fellowship and two Pushcart Prizes and has been a resident at Yaddo and a fellow at Bread Loaf. He lives with his wife, the poet Alessandra Lynch, and their two sons, Milo and Oliver, in Indianapolis, where he teaches at Butler University.

LAURA HARTENBERGER lives in Toronto. Her writing has appeared or is forthcoming in *The Massachusetts Review, Cutbank Magazine, Dragnet, Nano Fiction, Winter Tangerine Review,* and others, and has won prizes from *Gulf Coast Magazine* and *The Hart House Review*. She recently participated in *The Found Poetry Review*'s Pulitzer Remix project, where she produced thirty poems out of the 1933 Pulitzer-winning novel, *The Store*.

PAUL HAWKINS is a poet based in Bournemouth UK and an associate artist of Vita Nova. He curates a community storytelling project Untold Boscombe, and co-edits the Boscombe Revolution poetry pamphlet. Paul has performed his work at The Royal Opera House, WOMAD, The Shelley Theatre, and other venues and festivals across the UK. His publishing credits include *Rising, The Interpreters House, Stride, Fit to Work: Poets Against ATOS, The Occupy Wall Street Anthology, Primal Urge, London Lit Project*, The Bath Lit Festival, Museum of Alcohol, Verba Vitae, M58, and Lit Kicks. His pamphlet, *Claremont Road*, will be published by erbacce-press in early 2014. Preoccupied with words, alternative culture, music, and protest, Paul has moved about every eleven months, but has only ever owned one tent. He was nominated for a Pushcart prize in 2013.

DEBORAH HERMAN is an emerging poet with previous publications in *Existere, Rhythm, Transverse*, and *Vallum*.

SANDRA HERMAN studied fine arts and creative writing at York University. She has been exhibiting artwork in Toronto since 2007. Her first international contribution was displayed at the "USB Shuffle Show," at Abteilung Für Alles Andere, Berlin, in 2013.

MATHIAS JANSSON is a Swedish art critic and poet. He has been published in a variety of magazines, including *The Horror Zine Magazine, Dark Eclipse, Schlock, The Sirens Call,* and *The Poetry Box*. He has also contributed to anthologies from Horrified Press and James Ward Kirk Fiction, including *Suffer Eternal Anthology Volume 1-3, Hell Whore Anthology Volume 1-3, Barnyard Horror*, and *Serial Killers Tres Tria.* (Web: mathiasjansson72.blogspot.se)

JAX NTP holds an MFA in Creative Writing, Poetry, from Cal State University, Long Beach. She was the Editor-in-Chief of *RipRap Literary Journal Vol 35*, and won the William T. Shadden Scholarship Graduate Award for Poetry in 2013. Her work has been featured in *PEARL, 3AM (UK), Cordite (AU), The Mas Tequila Review, The Fat City Review, Subliminal Interiors, Moon Tide Press*, and *The Art of Survival.* (Website: jaxntp.tumblr.com)

ROSEMARIE KEENAN, with her husband and writing partner, Vince Keenan, is 2013 winner of the William F. Deeck Malice Domestic Grant for Unpublished Writers. Her poem "Holiday Hours" is scheduled for the December 23, 2013 issue of the online publication *The 5-2: Crime Poetry Weekly.*

WM. TODD KING is a poet and Regulatory Compliance Supervisor living in Kentucky. He is the recent recipient of the Elizabeth Lane Award, and was a participant in the 2013 *Pulitzer Remix* project. His works have appeared in *STILL, 4 and 20 Poetry, Life's Vivid Creations*, and *Found Poetry Review.*

JOSEPH LISOWSKI grew up under the shadow of Heppenstall Steel Mill in Pittsburgh, Pennsylvania, and has spent much of his life near the sea, including ten years in St. Thomas, VI, which serves as the setting for his three published mystery novels, *Full Body Rub, Looking for Lisa*, and *Looking for Lauren.* He has lived many lives: as a wide-eyed boy, a keeper of keys, a beachcomber. (There are poems somewhere commemorating them all.) Now he regularly bicycles along the banks of the Pasquotank River near the outer banks of North Carolina, where he and his wife Linda are professors at Elizabeth City State University. In 2013, he won the University of North Carolina Board of Governors Teacher of the Year Award. His most recent book of poetry is *Stashu Kapinski Dreams of Glory* (Sweatshoppe Publications, 2013).

RENEE MALLETT is a mostly okay dame who walks down mean streets at night packing heat and looking for trouble. Her prose, poetry, and creative nonfiction have been published in a number of journals both in print and online. She is also the author of a series of local interest books. Visit her online at ReneeMallett.com or in person the first Saturday of every month for Open Studios at Western Ave Studios in Lowell, Massachusetts.

ADRIAN MANNING writes from Leicester, England. His poetry and articles have appeared in numerous chapbooks, magazines, and on-line sites around the world. He is also the editor of Concrete Meat Press. His poetry appears in the Silver Birch Press *Bukowski Anthology*.

KAREN MARGOLIS was born in Harare, Zimbabwe, and educated in South Africa and London. She graduated as a mathematician in 1974 and has since moved mainly in the world of words as a freelance author, poet, journalist, editor, broadcaster, and translator. She has lived in Berlin since 1983. Her books include *To Eat or Not to Eat* (1988), and *The Floating Castle* (Kindle 2012), and she has published poems and essays in numerous anthologies and magazines. She is the translator from German into English of *The Art of Philosophy* by Peter Sloterdijk (2012), and *The Land of the Five Flavors: a Cultural History of Chinese Cuisine* by Thomas Hoellmann (2013), both published by Columbia University Press.

CATFISH MCDARIS has been active in the small press world for 250 years. He lives in a cave at a nudist colony. His biggest seller is *Prying: with Jack Micheline & Charles Bukowski*. His latest book is a hardcover called *Jupiter Orgasma* from Lulu.com.

MARCIA MEARA is a native Floridian, living in the Orlando area with her husband of twenty-seven years, two silly little dachshunds and four big, lazy cats. She's fond of reading, gardening, hiking, canoeing, painting, and writing, not necessarily in that order. But her favorite thing in the world is spending time with her two grandchildren, eight-year-old Tabitha Faye, and seven-month-old Kaelen Lake. Marcia is the author of *Wake-Robin Ridge*, a romantic suspense novel set in the beautiful Blue Ridge Mountains, and *Summer Magic: Poems of Life and Love*. She is currently working on her second novel, *Swamp Ghosts*, set alongside the wild and scenic rivers of central Florida. Her philosophy? It's never too late to follow your dream. Just take that first step, and never look back.

JAMES W. MOORE is a playwright and poet living in Winooski, Vermont. *I Am the Maker of all sweetened possum*, a collection of poems he created as part of Found Poetry Review's Pulitzer Remix, will be published by Silver Birch Press in 2014. Five of his plays have received world premieres in Portland, Oregon. Find him at jameswmoore.wordpress.com.

SARAH NICHOLS is a writer and artist living and working in Connecticut, and the author of *The Country of No* (Finishing Line Press, 2012). In April 2013, she participated in Pulitzer Remix, a National Poetry Month initiative, with eighty-four other writers, creating found poems out of the Pulitzer Prize winners for fiction. Her chapbook manuscript, *The Dream and Other Poems,* was recently named as a semifinalist in the *Paper Nautilus* Vella chapbook competition for 2013.

WINSTON PLOWES is the proud hoarder of an extended family of spiral bound notebooks. These books are the foster homes for forgotten words found in detective novels, sci-fi comics, and tabloid newspapers. Some were found lost on the street, ignored on public transport or abandoned in litterbins. He has recently found homes for his words in print publications such as *Turbulence magazine, The Best of Manchester Poets (Vol 3), Monkey Kettle, The Hebden Bridge Times* and *The Found Poetry Review.* In April 2013, he took part in the Online Pulitzer Remix project. Find out more by visiting his website winstonplowes.co.uk.

DAVID SCOTT POINTER the son of a piano playing bank robber who died when David was three years old. David later served in the Marine military police. He earned a B.S. degree in Criminal Justice and an M.A. in sociology. Recent poetry was published in *Rattle: Law Enforcement Tribute, J Journal: New Writings on Justice, 5-2 Crime Poetry Weekly, Indiana Crime Review, Serial Killers Iterium,* and elsewhere. His newest poetry book is *Oncoming Crime Facts.*

D.A. (DAVID) PRATT has often said that reading D.H. Lawrence's *Lady Chatterley's Lover* changed his life when he read the book in his later teens. Now he wonders how younger generations are going to experience this sort of thing, since responding to a series of text messages just isn't the same as reading a novel. Within the context that he knows why he is living in Regina, Saskatchewan, Canada, David continues to wonder why he continues to live in Regina, Saskatchewan, Canada. In 2013, his short piece of prose entitled "Encountering Bukowski—Some Canadian Notes" appeared in *Bukowski: An Anthology of Poetry & Prose About Charles Bukowski* published by Silver Birch Press and his essay entitled "The Five

Henry Millers" appeared in the tenth annual issue of *Nexus: The International Henry Miller Journal.*

DAVID RACHELS is the editor of *Redheads Die Quickly and Other Stories* (UP of Florida, 2012), the first collection of Gil Brewer's short fiction. He is a professor of English at Newberry College in Newberry, South Carolina.

JONNE RHODES, in her current work as a Natural Resource Volunteer with the California Department of Fish and Wildlife, coaches conflict prevention to the human half of coyote/human interactions. She performs dental work on American black bears, and patrols remote canyons. Jonne is a weekly participant in Donna Hilbert's Poetry Workshop in Long Beach, and contributed to the *Silver Birch Green Anthology.*

VAN ROBERTS is a writer, editor and the director of Little Raven Publishing, based in Melbourne, Australia.

DANIEL ROMO is the author of *When Kerosene's Involved* (Black Coffee Press, 2013) and *Romancing Gravity* (Silver Birch Press, 2013). His poetry and photography can be found in the *Los Angeles Review, Gargoyle, MiPOesias, Yemassee, Hobart,* and elsewhere. He holds an MFA from Queens University of Charlotte and teaches creative writing. He lives in Long Beach, California. More of his writing can be found at danielromo.net.

TERE SIEVERS lives and works in Long Beach, California. Born and raised on the Jersey shore, she finds inspiration in that East Coast past and this West Coast present. Her poems have appeared in *Pearl, Verve, Black Buzzard Review,* and the Silver Birch Press *Green Anthology* as well as "Your Daily Poem" online.

GERALD SO is a graduate of Hofstra University and Queens College/CUNY. Since 1999, he has moderated online forums about crime fiction, film, and television. From 2001-2009, he edited the first-run short fiction section of thrillingdetective.com. Currently, Gerald edits The 5-2: Crime Poetry Weekly at poemsoncrime.blogspot.com.

SHERRY STEINER lives in Housatonic, Massachusetts, and is originally from New York City. She is a published writer of offbeat poetry, monologues, flash fiction, and musical performance pieces, as well as an Arts Educator, exhibiting visual artist, and more. For detailed background information: sherrysteiner.com.

CAITLIN STERN grew up in San Antonio, Texas, where she read in trees, avoided team sports, and "published" her first book in elementary school. As she grew, she wrote and read more, developing into an avid bibliophile and writer. She followed her love of books to Angelo State University, where she worked as a tutor at her school's Writing Center, and later as a Teaching Assistant while she earned an English MA. During 2013, she edited an e-published mystery novel, and several of her poems were published in the Silver Birch Press *Summer Anthology*.

SCOTT STOLLER's poems have appeared in many journals and anthologies including *Weave, Prick of the Spindle, decomP* and *Take Five*. He's been nominated for the & Now Award for Best Innovative Writing, and lives in the west suburbs of Chicago.

THOMAS R. THOMAS was born in Los Angeles and grew up in the San Gabriel Valley west of LA. Currently, he lives in Long Beach, California. For his day job, he is a software QA Analyst. He volunteers for Tebot Bach, a community poetry organization, in Huntington Beach. Thomas has been published in *Don't Blame the Ugly Mug: 10 Years of 2 Idiots Peddling Poetry, Creepy Gnome, Carnival, Pipe Dream, Bank Heavy Press, Conceit Magazine, Electric Windmill & Marco Polo,* and the Silver Birch Press *Summer Anthology*. In November 2012, Carnival released his eChapbook, *Scorpio*, and Washing Machine Press released a chapbooklette called *Tanka*. In October 2013, World Parade Books published a book of his poetry, *Five Lines*. Visit the author's website at thomasrthomas.org.

MARY UMANS is a filmmaker and writer living in New York City. Her short film, *The Braddock Boys*, was featured in the 2012 Manhattan Film Festival.

MELANIE VILLINES is a novelist, playwright, screenwriter, television writer, biographer, editor, and ghostwriter. Her published work includes the novel *Tales of the Sacred Heart* (Bogfire Press), the family memoir *Reason to Fight* (co-written with Hiram Johnson), a celebrity biography *Beyond Hollywood* (co-written with J. Herbert Klein), *Anna & Otto*, a novel for children (Inklings Press), and a variety of ghostwritten books and screenplays. A founding member of Chicago Dramatists, she is the author of twenty plays. Her original screenplays include *Calling Oz*, finalist in the Austin Film Festival and many other screenwriting competitions, and *Just Say the Word*, top-10 finalist in Illinois-Chicago screenwriting competition. She co-wrote the critically acclaimed 90-minute drama *Crime of Innocence*, based on the life of Emmett Till, for the NBC affiliate in Chicago. Her play *Bernice* (co-written with Hiram Johnson and Jessica Everleth) had a February 2013 workshop production in Dallas, and her story "Windy City Sinners," an excerpt from her upcoming novel of the same name, appeared in the *Chicago Quarterly Review* Vol. 17/2014.

MERCEDES WEBB-PULLMAN: Mercedes Webb-Pullman graduated from IIML Victoria University Wellington New Zealand MA in Creative Writing 2011. Her work appears online and in print *(Danse Macabre, Turbine, 4th Floor, Swamp, Reconfigurations, The Electronic Bridge, poetryrepairs, Connotations Press, The Red Room, anthologies, and her books Ono, Looking for Kerouac, After the Danse, Numeralla Dreaming,* and *Food 4 Thought)* She lives on the Kapiti Coast, New Zealand, and is Lazarus Media LLC's Assistant Editor, Pacific, and Editor-in-Chief, DM du Jour.

RICHARD WINK is a writer from Norwich, England. He has written two collections of poetry, *Dead End Road* (BeWrite Books 2009) and *Gord* (Horror Sleaze Trash Press, 2012). He regularly contributes various rants, reviews, and interviews to a variety of zines, rags, websites, and periodicals.

JOANIE HIEGER FRITZ ZOSIKE is a writer, actor, singer, director, and arts in education presenter. Her work has appeared in such publications as *Chez Chez, clockwise.wordpress.com 2012, Helicon Nine, Heresies, International Worker, Jewish Daily Forward, La Mia Ink, Maintenant, Ovation,* Silver Birch Press *Summer Anthology, Womannews,* and *Zeitriss* (Augsburg, Germany). Barncott Press (London) will release her poetry collection, *An Alphabet of Love* and *Sleep,* in ebook and print versions in early 2014, and in spring 2014 her work will appear in *At the Edge.* A veteran of The Living Theatre, she directs the dada/surrealist company, DADAnewyork, and is cofounder and codirector of *Action Racket Theatre* in New York City. In December 2014, she will appear in *A Christmas Carol* at the Abingdon Square Theatre in New York City (with Austin Pendleton as Scrooge). She is currently working on a science fantasy novel and her fifth full-length play.

ABOUT THE COVER ARTIST

Born in Dearborn, Michigan, **Guy Budziak** has spent most of his life living in and around Detroit. He attended Wayne State University in the mid/late 1980s as a fine arts major with a concentration in painting. It wasn't until 1999 that he switched from painting to print-making, specifically woodcuts, at a time he was immersing himself in all things noir, books as well as films. His first piece, completed in 1999, was an image from Jacques Tourneur's *Out of the Past*. A few years later, Roger Ebert, a great fan of the film, bought a print. In 2008, Budziak's image of Alain Delon in Jean-Pierre Melville's 1967 neo-noir *Le Samourai* appeared on the cover of Ginette Vincendeau's book, *Les Stars et le Star-Systeme en France* (*The Stars and the Star-System in France*), published by L'Harmattan. In 2012, *Giuseppina Magazine* published a six-page spread spotlighting his work. Learn more at filmnoirwoodcuts.com.

www.ingramcontent.com/pod-product-compliance
Lightning Source LLC
Chambersburg PA
CBHW070638030426
42337CB00020B/4070